A TRUE SOUL

poems

HELENA BORDEN

Braughler™
Books

Cover photo: 123RF/rsndetre

Printed in the United States of America
Published by Braughler Books LLC., Springboro, Ohio
First printing, 2022
ISBN: 978-1-955791-53-3

Library of Congress Control Number: 2022919237

Ordering information: Special discounts are available on quantity purchases by bookstores, corporations, associations, and others. For details, contact the publisher at: sales@braughlerbooks.com or at 937-58-BOOKS.

For questions or comments about this book, please write to: info@braughlerbooks.com

Braughler™ Books
braughlerbooks.com

To everyone who believed in me and to those who did not, here I am.

To my teachers, friends, family, animals, church, and support team, thank you.

To anyone who has ever wanted to quit. Your voice matters. You matter.

To families grieving the loss of loved ones. To those who have no one.

To those who feel like an outcast, those who feel unlovable, those who have been left by everyone.

To my readers: never stop believing in your dreams, they may seem far but with faith and perseverance great things can happen.

Finally, to my great-grandma, you were only in my life for four short years but your love is a legacy.

Contents

A TRUE SOUL

DESPAIR

Her mind was constantly racing
Her body was consistently pacing.
She knew she was loved, but no love she felt.
Empty, broken, lost—described her constant feelings.
She said her flaws repeatedly—day and night, the cycle
    repeating.
And although she could say she was good, she was smart,
    she was funny
Down in her heart, she didn't believe a word spoken.

She gave love to everyone around her,
But she couldn't muster the smallest amount of love for
    herself.
She grew up too fast.
Her father abandoned her; her mother struggled
She was an adult—the thought of being a child was
    foreign.
She forced a smile on her face,
Always saying she was okay.
Nobody knew the amount of pain she went through
The nights she cried herself to sleep.
The blood that dripped on her arms
The wish of death she constantly thought.

She knew she had a future.
In her heart she longed for a family, to be a mother,
To give love and receive love.
There was a God more powerful than her
There was a plan for her future
There was hope for the broken soul.

In the quiet moment of night, all she felt was despair.
She felt alone.
She knew there was a reason to push on
But she was stuck in the dark.

COUNTRY DRIVING

She was driving.
Country music in her ears
Wind blowing in her hair
Tears falling down her face.

She knew she could
She could drive forever.
But the what ifs stopped her.
What if she ran out of gas
What if there was an accident
What if her engine broke.

Things that never happened, stopped her.
She was stuck in the mud.
She was losing control.
Everyone around her kept driving by
They didn't see the car spinning and flipping.

She prayed. She cried.
She saw her life flash before her eyes.
Just when she thought she was gone,
An angel guided her tires
She was right-side up
She was in control on the road.

She soared down her lane
Her tears dried as the wind hit her face
Her voice carried through the country roads.
She was free. She was fine.
She was driving.

FREEDOM IS A RACE

Some Days you're gonna rise
Some Days you're gonna fall
Some Days it will feel like you're nothing at all.
Remember life is like a race.
Sometimes you get ahead,
Sometimes you fall short,
But most importantly,
Always keep a smile on your face.

Figure out who you are,
And remember precious one,
Your friends are with you
Both near and far.

Don't give up now
You've come so far
You have so long to go,
Life may be low
And it may feel slow,
But look towards the future,
You've got so much ahead.
You may not see it now,
But somehow,
Somehow, things will be great.

A FRIEND

The sun goes down
The moon comes up.
You expect a smile,
All you see is a frown.

They scream and yell
You go to your room
You've got no-one to tell.
You feel like crap,
But then you feel a gentle tap.
You turn and look
Your friend is right there
You hug them,
Cry in their hair,
They sit and listen
And at that moment,
You know they truly care.

GROWING UP

Some people grow up:
They stop lying
They stop hurting
They stop drinking
They escape past their fears.

Some people stay stuck.
Drinking, smoking, cutting
Never seeing the light at the end of the tunnel.

You are blessed.
You can choose to live in the blessing
Or you can stay in the darkness,
Never experiencing happiness.

Those fake smiles, fake words
They make up your life but you decide what happens.
It may seem impossible but it doesn't have to stay like that.

Yes, you are broken, everyone is, life is
But you can put the pieces back together
You are valued and those pieces that are broken aren't lost.
You can grow up or you can stay stuck in the dark.

THE FAITH WE NEED

Faith.
You can't see it
You can't hold it
You can live with it.

It saves you from falling
Makes the hard days a little easier.
The twinkling light you see in the dark
The energy you get when you feel like giving up.

Faith.
Something born within you that you learn to trust.
A feeling you hold on to when you want to give up.

It makes you hold on
It gives you life
It gives you something to trust in that will never fail.

Born of spirit, died a man
Faith. Belief. Salvation.
The components that don't make life easy,
But make life something that you CAN get through.

Faith is in you.
Faith is for you.
Faith is with you.
Faith—something we all need.

PAIN

Bang my head against the wall
The bruises form, the pain flows through my head.
Cut deeper. The blood gushes out.
I just want to give up, but I can't.

My friends, my family,
What about them? Their feelings?
Mom is scared to talk to me,
Fearful I will act in anger on myself.

I just want to be held.
I just want someone to give me a hug.
Notice the fake smiles, the tears held in.
The pain I stuff so deep inside.

I've scared so many people off
Why would anyone want to stay?
I'm broken, lost, scared, afraid, scarred.
What will I ever accomplish?

In the quiet night, in the early morning,
I want someone to stay.
I don't want to scare them off.
I want them to want to love me.
I want to put my broken pieces back together.

CHURCH

Take me back to my church.
Take me to the pews, The laughs, the stories,
Communion Sundays, candle lit services, the Bible verses.
Take me back to the church.

Take me back to grace.
Forgive my sins, set me free.
I am a broken soul needing the savior.

Take me back to the hymns,
Arms raised, voices carrying throughout.
Take me back to my baptism.
Give me new life through the water of the spirit.

Take me back to my Lord.
Wrap me in his arms, feeling his love so freely.
Let him dry my tears, holding me close.

Take me back to my faith,
The stories we heard in Sunday school
The games we played in the evenings
The new life given freely to us all.

Take me back to the church.
My home, my comfort, my life,
My friend, my soul, the place of forgiveness.
New life, grace, and all of the faith I've ever needed.

Church of heaven take me back.

POWERLESS TO POWER

Powerless was how she felt.
falling into a dark tunnel with no sense of what would
    happen.
She screamed, she cried, but her voice was silent.

She was a resilient young lady.
Earned good grades, made others smile and laugh.
In her deepest hardships, she put others first,
allowing the pain that couldn't speak engulf her.

Others saw her successes, her moments of greatness,
all of her fears, worries, pains, aches, and temptations
    hidden.
She wanted to be the girl they saw in her,
not the girl she saw in herself.

She wanted to be happy, healthy, and live a prosperous life.
She wanted to live in the truth that others spoke,
most importantly though—
live in the truth her heavenly father gave her.

She proclaimed the gospel,
lived a life for the one who died for her.
She defeated darkness with angels by her side,
And at last, when all was well with her soul,
Heaven took her home and she fell to her father's arms.

Powerless she felt no more,
more than ever she felt powerful.
She was saved by grace, given new life,
and finally she was the girl he saw in her that she always
    wanted to be.

HEAVENLY TOUCH

She didn't know love, but love was given immensely to her.
She was held close, her fears gone.
The arms that held her called her their daughter
their artwork, their creation made beautifully.

She felt peace, comfort, a sense of safety she had never
    experienced.
"I have walked with you, I always will"
"You are my daughter, the one I made to live in my image"
The voice whispered to her;
it was a quiet and soothing voice.
Her heavenly father held her and nothing could hurt her.

A QUIET PRAYER

The leaves falling, the sky a purple blue.
She drove into the night
Her mind was at ease,
Her fears gone,
Her body at peace with the night.

She prayed as she drove,
a prayer she often prayed—
God, you are with me
I surrender all to you,
Call me home at your wish and I will come
Protect me on this Earth
Bring peace and happiness like never before. Amen.

The spirit was in her,
it moved her forward, kept her on track.
The spirit lived in her
It shined through her sharing His love.
She was a messenger, sharing the great word
The word that would protect her when she failed.

TOGETHER

Some friends are there for years,
some are there for special moments,
times of struggle and doubt.
The best friends you can have are your friends in Christ.

You walked into my life at a dark time,
You prayed, we cried, we laughed,
you were older but it didn't matter,
We were friends and would get through the good and bad.

you make me laugh, you make me smile,
when life gets hard I come to you
and although you cannot take the pain away,
you can sit with me and be there.

Many people leave, not you
you came, you stayed.
Best friends aren't about quantity but quality;
having you as my friend is the best,
better than twenty fake friends.

You support me,
I support you,
Most importantly, we both are supported by our creator,
We grow in his love
together we get through the valleys of evil and shadows of
    death.

DEAR YOUNG ONE...

Young one...
there will be times of struggle,
times of despair, times of fear.
You'll want to give up,
You'll want to quit,
You'll want to throw it all away.

Don't give up now,
persevere, fight, stand strong,
You are wise,
You are smart,
You are blessed and protected.
You can make it through the hard times.

Young one...
I'll always be with you,
I'll hold your hand, guiding you in the dark.
I'll stay close, I'll sing your song of peace.

Young one...
The world is evil,
You will be hated,
You will be teased,
You will want to quit.

I can't stop you, I have to let you go,
But young one...
Know I will always be with you
And you are never alone.

A FEELING

Her desire for death was strong,
so was her wish to live.
stuck in a battle between life and death
she felt as though she was sinking.
Her emotions were battling her logic,
her actions battling her morals.
How would she ever grow out of it?
Would it ever end?
The war continued, day and night.
"Please!" she cried out.
She didn't want to give up,
she didn't want to quit
She didn't know what to do.

The words, the cuts, the blood,
the tears, the darkness—
it engulfed her.
She felt like she was going to quit.
Scared of herself, she cried
she hid.
Running to her teacher, and counselor, and pastor,
and friend, and dog, and God... she cried.
She just wanted the pain to be gone,
even for a moment.
one singular moment.
"Why?" she asked.
She was a girl with a smile,
hiding the pain behind the sparkles in her eyes
and the giggles in her voice.

SUMMER

Summer...
children laughing, sunshine in the sky,
the voice of a parent calling their young one home.
For many, summer is a time of fun,
relaxation, stress free—a time to be yourself.
For many though, summer is darkness.
evil lurks, thoughts creep into the mind,
memories flood the banks, the hills grow taller,
the sky gets darker.
Time at home, time with family,
time alone, time with thoughts;
the worst of them all.
Summer,
a time some see as beautiful, others see as darkness.
the ends couldn't repel more,
the feelings couldn't shake any more emotions.
For summer,
a time that so many take for granted—
the hungry mouths, the crying eyes, the broken souls.
Many hate school, but for some, school is their summer.
A break, a time to focus, a time to feel accomplished.
Summer can be fun but stressful.
Remember those who don't follow the crowd,
the sick, the hurting, the abused,
the ones who for them,
school is their summer and summer is their hell.

THANK YOU

You have watched me grow,
wrapped your arms around me in my time of need,
believed in me when I didn't believe in myself.

Summer will be hard
but the memories I will hold close.
I will remember our laughs, our tears,
the way you cared about me.
when I first met you, I was scared,
I hid, I was mean, I built a wall,
the wall getting bigger every time I saw you.

One day, I let the wall down,
It was one of the best decisions of my life.
You led me in my faith,
you led me in life,
summer will be hard without you,
For now though, I want to celebrate all we have
        accomplished.
You got me through the darkest of valleys, the scariest of
        mountains.
My final words to you are THANK YOU!

TO MY LOVE

This isn't goodbye,
It's just for a short time.
Darling, I will always be a phone call away,
a text in the night, a drive down the highway.
Love, you mean the world to me.
Never forget that.
You're beautiful, special, caring,
Darling, I love you...
I always have.
You are my world, my sunshine.
You are my moon bringing night and rest.
You are my life, my purpose,
without you, life is bare,
empty, full of despair.
Although I can't touch you,
I can't see you,
I know you are always there.
You're always one call away,
one short drive down the highway,
one knock at the door,
one text that says
"I love you".

UNWANTED

Rest. Sit. Stay.
It's all they say.
They want me to be someone I'm not.
They want me to be perfect,
their perfect child, one they could be proud of.

I wasn't good enough as my own self.
I was too quiet, too loud;
too smart, not smart enough;
too caring, not caring enough;
good, but not good enough.
I tried ever so hard.
Sitting with my eyes closed I imagined:
I was a strong, independent girl that pleased everyone.
I was smart, funny, had a good job, caring,
and was good enough for me and everyone else.

I came back to reality with a hard slap.
"Why do you just sit?" they yelled.
I got up, my life's purpose was to serve them,
to be the girl they wanted me to be.
That night, the feelings became too much.
With tears in my eyes I wrote my last words—
"I hope you are happy, I was not.
The daughter you didn't want is gone,
so is the one you longed to have".
The chair fell and all was over.
Their precious imperfect daughter was gone.

MY CHILD

Dear child,
life will be hard, you will fall,
there will be bruises and cuts
remember I'll always love you through it all.

You'll run away from me;
shout, yell, scream
I'll still love you.
Remember my quiet voice in the loud storm:
"I will be with you always till the end of the age".
You are my child,
my daughter, my perfectly imperfect creation.

Find peace in me— hope, joy,
a feeling of love greater than any other.
Surrender all to me and everything will be okay.
Yes, there will still be evil,
I can't take that away,
but I can reassure you that you will live forever,
you will find happiness
you will live an amazing life.

Dearest one, my daughter,
You will live an awesome life,
I will be with you in so many ways; so many forms.
I am a whisper in the wind,
a knock at the door,
I am here for you now and forever.

Daughter, you will be okay.
I love you forever and always.
Daughter, I will protect you,
run to my arms and I'll hold you.
Dearest one, my precious daughter
you are imperfectly perfect,
but remember I'll love you through it all.
Sincerely, me.

BECAUSE...

Because of you I sing a little louder,
smile a little brighter,
dance a little bolder.

Because of you I dry my tears,
I cry in laughter instead of sadness,
I come out of hiding instead of hiding in fear.

Because of you I have made it to where I am today
My days may be numbered,
but because of you, those numbers go to infinity.

Because of you, each day I wake up with a purpose,
my ashes brought to life,
my darkness glowing with a light brighter than the sun.

Because of you, I am not done.
I push through every day
I make everything count.

Because of you I sing a little louder,
smile a little brighter,
dance a little bolder.

Because of you, I am a better me.

THE MASKED GIRL

Thorough, detailed, inspiring,
the life of the young girl.
She went from town to town,
pleasing others,
always striving to be better.
The story of a young girl—
a girl nobody really knew.

She appeared outgoing, intelligent, creative,
inside she was the opposite.
She was a quiet yet bright young mind.
Nobody saw past the masks, the scars,
everyone saw the girl they wanted,
not the girl she wanted to be.

Yes, she wanted to make others happy,
but her dying wish was to be truly happy herself.
She put others first, forgetting herself who she was.
The girl everyone saw,
the girl everyone else wanted,
was the girl she had become.

DEPRESSION

Hide it. Be happy. Smile.
"Shhh" it's a secret,
Nobody talks about it in public.

Many understand it,
but we all must still keep it quiet.
The scars, the hurting, the racing thoughts.

quick! everyone put on a mask
"I'm fine" rings in the air
Whatever happened to being honest,
asking for help?
Wait, you stopped it.
You had to become a secret.

Depression,
you had to hide,
nobody could know you were with me.

The laughs, the whispers,
being seen with you is like swimming naked in a public pool.

Oh depression,
I wish others saw our real relationship.
Sadly, we must keep it a secret.
It is better for me that way.

oh wait, or is it?

FIGHT

The panic,
the sirens.
The pain.
I wake up sweating.
It was just a dream,
just a dream I tell myself.

Except, it wasn't.
The pain, the abuse, the scars,
they're all real,
they all happened.

I can run, I can hide,
I can't change the past.
I can grow or stay stuck.

The pain and fear can engulf me,
or I can fight and stand my battle ground.

Fight. Fight. I am strong.
I will get through this,
the pain won't last forever.

Fight. Fight. I will grow.
The pain isn't me,
I decide who I am,
I decide my future,
not you or the pain you caused.

TAKE ME HOME

Bells ringing, the choir singing.
Take me back to my home.
The prayers, the friends.

I'm tired of the masking,
the hiding, the fear.
Take me back to my home.

My father lives there,
my brother and sisters.
Take me back to my family,
the ones who really care.

I'm tired of the pain,
the suffering, the never-ending sin.
God, take me back.
I wanna go home.

Take me to eternal peace,
life everlasting,
an infinite life with you.

God, bring me home to heaven.

TO BE A CHILD

She was always playing,
running, smiling, giggling, pretending.

Oh to be a child.
The carelessness,
the freedom,
the innocence from the evil world.

to be a child again would be a rebirth,
a new life, a second chance.

I would smile more,
giggle louder,
play all of my days away.

Fight the naps,
enjoy the freedoms,
remember the innocence.

soak in the Love from everyone around.
always being complimented,
not having a care in the world.

Oh to be a child, the things I would do again and again.

SHOUT IT. FIGHT IT. VOICE IT.

shout for joy
shout for freedom
shout for a voice
shout for justice
shout for equality
shout for your beliefs.

The hiding, the quietness,
never will change happen.

Fight.
Fight for yourself
Fight for those who don't have a voice
Fight for those who have a voice but don't use it

The hiding, the quietness,
Change it. Voice it. Speak it.
Live it.

A voiceless voice voices nothing.
A silent changer changes nothing.
A defeated fighter wins nothing.

Fight it.
Voice it.
Change it.

You have the power so use it.

HEAD AND HEART

From the head to the heart,
thoughts flowing,
feelings flowing,
emotions flowing.

continuously they flow,
round and round they go
from the head to the heart
the heart to the head.

See, the problem lies there.
from the heart to the head,
emotions over logic,
then the head to the heart
logic over emotions.

Never a balance,
the balance that would still the universe
quiet the raging storms,
control the urges you ever so long to do.

From the head to the heart
the heart to the head...

No! From the head AND the heart.

PRAYER

I prayed for you
young one,
someone cares,
I am someone,
I care.

I prayed for you daughter,
your parents love you
they are people who love;
they love you.

I prayed for you sister,
you are my sister,
the one I am supposed to protect
we may argue, but sister I love you.

I prayed for you pastor.
You pray for me,
the favor should be returned.

People of all races, ages, cultures,
I prayed for you.
You are loved.
You have a purpose even when it feels like there is none.

Remember my prayer for you.
Always remember how I prayed for you.

HER STORY

If she only knew...
knew how much she was loved,
how valued she was,
how important her purpose was.

If she only knew....
knew that she writes her own story
knew that her pain and past doesn't define her.

If she only knew...
knew her life was bigger than herself
her story would save others
her pain would make her fiercer.

If she only knew...
knew not to quit,
that her life would be amazing
The best was yet to come.

If she only knew...
knew the love given to her,
the pain she caused when she hurt herself
the eternal life she was promised.

If she only knew....
if they only knew...
if you only knew...

A PERFECT WORLD

I could only imagine.
leaves falling
purplish-blue sky.
a perfect world.
A world with no evil
no sin, no shame.

Everyone would be happy.
and leaves would fall
and the weather would be a crisp cool 70 degrees
and sunshine everyday
and the wind blowing in my hair.

The perfect family—
a brother and sister and two parents.
Friends aplenty
and smiles all around.

The perfect world,
a world only one can dream of.

MY GOD

For you are with me,
nothing can stand against me.
My father's love,
greater than anything you could find,
the infinite power beyond any other.

The grace, forgiveness, being saved
only he can do it.
Only my father
my provider
my protector
my creator.

For with his strength I am armored.
By his grace I am forgiven
With his love I can love indefinitely.

Oh God,
my father, my parent, my provider,
how sweet the sound of your voice
how comforting your loving touch.

For when you are with me,
nothing…. Nothing is impossible.

ANXIETY

The beeping
the voices
the thoughts
the people
the feelings
everything is too much.

Breathe they say;
 I can't!
The world is spinning
my heart is racing.
Please! Please! Please!

There is only one hope,
one solution,
one answer…

I just have to trust and surrender
something anxiety can't do.

FRIENDS

In and out of your life
like leaves on a river,
money in your bank.
Friends.
some stay for a while
others have a short visit.

Some make you laugh,
some make you smile,
some bless your life more than you know.

Friends support you,
they love you,
you love them.

Are you a friend?
Am I?

Friends...
you need them,
they need you
you need each other.

Friends...
The very thing that everyone needs.

GOD

My heart is overwhelmed,
my mind is racing
The thoughts flow constantly
one and then another and another.
I pray to you—
God of Jacob,
Father, Son, spirit, friend...
Lead me to a rock higher than I
Calm my soul
wash my heart and mind
renew me as your child.

Give me strength to stand when I fall,
rest when I am weary,
hope when my hope is empty.

I trust you.
I believe in you.
You believe in me.
So I pray to you oh God,
day and night

fearful or strong,
hopeless or hopeful,
lost or found in you.
I give it all to You.

NOT GOOD ENOUGH

The best I am just isn't enough
the tears, the mistakes—all I am.
My best isn't good enough,
for you or for anyone.

I try so hard,
I do the best I can
with all that I am
but it isn't good enough.

Nobody understands how hard I'm trying,
the moments I want to quit,
the days I don't want to get up.

I am just a failure;
a mistake to so many.
an invisible soul full of so much light.
a light that nobody wants to see.

I have an idea of what matters
the love, compassion, joy,
but to everyone else,
the physical work,
the person they want me to be
is just not good enough.

SURRENDER. FAITH. OVERCOMING.

Surrender— such a powerful word
I want to surrender,
I need to surrender,
What happens if I surrender?

Faith—an invisible trust that is visible to those around you
I want faith.
I need faith.
What happens when you have a faith greater than your
    own?

Overcoming— proving you are stronger than your battles.
I want to overcome my struggles.
I need to overcome my past.
Who will I be when I have overcome the mountains and
    valleys?

God— my overcomer, my faith, the one I surrender all to.
I want to hear you, God.
I need you God.
What will you make of my story God?
Who will I be when I surrender all to you?
What will happen when I put my faith in you?

LOVE

She loves all,
but has a hard time loving herself.
If she trusts you,
love her like you've never loved before.

Surround her in your arms
kiss her with love
hold her close.

Take her heart if she gives it to you,
never hurt her,
never abandon her,
Her love is the strongest earthly love of all.

Make her smile,
brush her hair,
tell her how much you need her,
how she is the best thing that you have ever had.

If she trusts you,
If she loves you,
that love will last forever.
It will be a love that nothing can break.

GIVING UP

Be strong young one,
darkness is defeated,
good overcame evil,
and you can overcome your past.

You can be a victim or a victory,
a disaster or a story full of mountains and valleys.
A struggle or a triumphiantry.

Young one,
don't give up on yourself now,
you've come so far,
you've seen so much,
been through hell and back,
but young one,
Your story will save lives.
you can overcome your struggles,
for you don't bear your cross alone,
There are many along the way to help.

Stay positive,
stay focused,
because young one,
you matter.
Your story is valued.
You have a purpose.
You are worth the fight.

CALLING OUT

faith is an anchor and trust is a journey
forgiveness is an act and hope is a state of mind.

having faith is trusting that you will be okay
trust is believing that he will protect you

Forgiveness is relieving the pain you carry on your cross
Hope is a part of it all— something that everyone needs.

Crying out in pain, sorrow, depression, hatred,
faith answers, forgiveness removes the anger,
trust restores,
 Hope renews your faith, your life, your future.

call out and he will answer—
That is faith, hope, and trust.
shout to him your stories,
your past, your mistakes—
His answer is forgiveness.

The lord your God,
your friend, protector, father…
He is faith.
He is hope.
He is forgiveness.
He is trust.
He is everything.

BUYING A CAR

She was free,
The hard work had paid off.
she flew down the road,
wind in her hair,
music blasting for her soul.

The money,
the times people told her she never could,
the doubters,
the people who bullied her into wanting to give up...

she made it past them,
past the doubt,
the insecurities,
the flaws.

She was free.
Life consisted of just three things now:
Herself, God, and her Car.

SEEING GOD

The morning was dark,
I arose in the hospital bed
aware of the pain I was in.

That morning,
that dark and dusky morning,
I saw God.

I had read the book,
knew the stories,
seen the miracles,
but never believed.

That morning,
I saw God.
His hand on my heart,
his arms wrapped around me.

I saw God that day.
bright and early,
that morning my life changed
Why?

Because I saw God that day.

DARKNESS

surrounded in the darkness,
carrying the weight of the world,
she sobbed.
"Why?" she cried out.
Why was she alone?
Why could she help others while hurting herself?
Who was she?

The masks,
the fake "I'm fine",
it was all becoming too much.
She wanted to quit.
Nobody would care anyway
her friends were few and far
her family seemed like a puzzle;
one that she couldn't seem to put the pieces together to.

 She cried, she lashed out, she hid,
nothing would release all of the emotions she had bottled
    inside.
she called out,
nobody answered.
you see,
she saw the pain of everyone else—
the hurting, the sorrow, the anger,
But nobody saw the pain she had—
The pain she tried so hard to ease.

BEAUTY

Beauty.
Wait, no ugly.
She hated the way she looked.
God told her she was so much—
beautiful, compassionate, caring, unique.
All she saw was the ugliness.

She was beautiful right?
No, by the world's standards she wasn't.
She was ugly, stupid, a coward.

Beauty is on the inside though
or so she thought.
The world hated her, so she must hate herself.

The scale told her she was overweight,
The kids laughed,
The clothes hugged her skin.

So…
She was ugly then, right?
No! She is beautiful.

beautiful in her own ways.
beautiful to her true friends
beautiful in the heart,
and beautiful to her heavenly father
the one whose opinion is held at the most high.

LATER

I once questioned life;
my future, my job, my friends, my purpose.
Life always seemed muddy,
impossible to make clean.

one day a boy asked me a question.
He said: What are those marks on you?
I held back the tears,
the memories flooded back.
"Later" I said.

"Later" it always was.
the answers, my story, the good,
everything was always later.

'Later" described my life.
what was and what would come to be.
I would always find out things later.
finish projects later,
cut out the cutting later.
start my life over later.

One day I realized, realized so many things:
my story wasn't supposed to be rewrote, it was just
        beginning
the cutting had to stop now,
the relationships had to be rebuilt
forgiveness had to happen.

It took a long time to realize because everything was "later".
My advice to you:
make your "later" now.

EMOTIONS

Peace.
The sand in your toes,
the waves crashing against the rocks.
everything was at peace—
your body, your mind, your soul.

Anger.
the rage in your voice,
yelling and arguing flooding the room.
Anger was all that was felt—
anger in your heart, mind, and body.

Joy.
The smile on your face,
the tears of laughter shed between friends.
joy and happiness were all around-
joy in your heart, happiness in your soul.

Sadness.
The gloomy darkness overtaking you.
the tears shed, the blood gushing.
sadness, dreariness, depression…
your mind, soul, and body covered by darkness.

A CHILD AGAIN

Dancing, singing,
the church bells ringing.

She was a child again.
Once lost but now was found.
She was freed,
the shackles undone by grace.
Her soul made new,
her heart grew,
her eyes were opened,
the Lord had spoken.

She believed—
believed in herself, her faith, and in others.
She loved all,
Forgave herself and others who had hurt her.

the amazing grace,
the triumphant shouts,
all rang in her ears,
as she danced about.

She was given new life,
rebirth, a second chance.
The lost one was saved,
The child was brought home.

Running into his arms,
as he wrapped her close,
she had finally found love, true love
true hope, true purpose, and true life.

NEW LIFE

Rebirth.
Rejoicing.
renewal.
I am made new because of you.

My smile shines brighter,
my laugh is a little louder,
My life is amazingly better.

I am happy,
I can be myself without fear,
I am proud
I am your child
I am unique
I am me.

Because of you,
your death and resurrection,
I am made new.
My past is behind me,
My future is bright.

Because of you,
I am a better me,
a new me,
the real me.

HELENA BORDEN is a young writer from the area of Fairfield Ohio. From an early age, she always had a passion for writing and helping other people, along with many other things. She is a straight-A student involved in her High School Wind ensemble, where she plays the flute and piccolo. She is also a member of the National Honor Society and Marching Band, and she regularly attends community events. Helena has a love for music, writing, and animals and is deeply rooted in her faith. Helena's inspirations for her book come from her own struggles and the desire to inspire others facing challenging times to find an outlet in writing. In her free time, she enjoys being in nature, spending with her friends, volunteering at animal rescues and her church, and most importantly helping anyone she can. She loves to read and write—her favorite types of books are poetry, autobiographies, critical thinking, and historical fiction. Helena hopes to inspire other young authors, as well as continuing to pursue her passion for writing in her own future.

www.ingramcontent.com/pod-product-compliance
Lightning Source LLC
LaVergne TN
LVHW052039080426
835513LV00018B/2387